THE MUMMY ANIMAL BOOK

Also by Jennifer Cossins

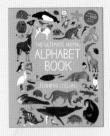

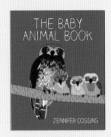

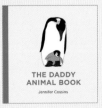

THE MUMMY ANIMAL BOOK

Jennifer Cossins

LOTHIAN
Children's Books

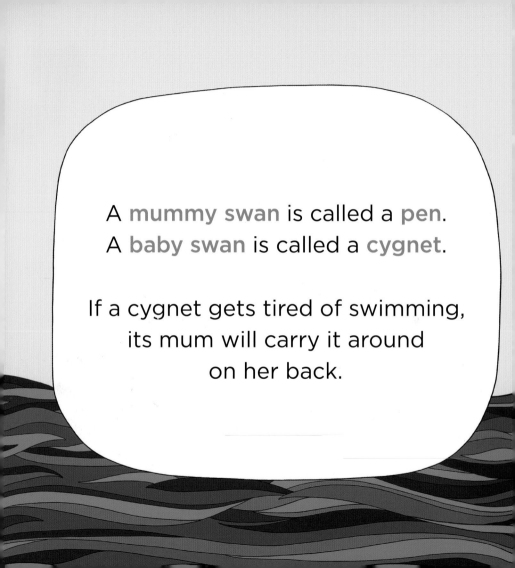

A **mummy swan** is called a **pen**.
A **baby swan** is called a **cygnet**.

If a cygnet gets tired of swimming,
its mum will carry it around
on her back.

A **mummy lion** is called a **lioness**.
A **baby lion** is called a **cub**.

Lionesses do most of the hunting for their pride and teach their cubs how to hunt.

A mummy elephant is called a cow.
A baby elephant is called a calf.

A calf will sometimes suck on its trunk just like a baby sucks its thumb.

A **mummy deer** is called a **doe**.
A **baby deer** is called a **fawn**.

Before it is even one hour old,
a fawn will take its first steps.

A **mummy cat** is called a **queen**.
A **baby cat** is called a **kitten**.

A kitten's eyes are always blue at first, but usually change colour later.

A **mummy goat** is called a **nanny**.
A **baby goat** is called a **kid**.

When a nanny gives birth to
her kids it's called 'kidding'.

A mummy fox is called a vixen.
A baby fox is called a kit.

When a kit is born, it can't see,
hear or walk, and is completely
dependent on its mum.

A **mummy donkey** is called a **jenny**.
A **baby donkey** is called a **foal**.

A jenny is pregnant for 365 days
and gives birth to one foal.

A **mummy kangaroo** is called a **flyer**.
A **baby kangaroo** is called a **joey**.

A joey dives into its mum's
pouch headfirst and must do a
somersault to flip upright again.

A mummy wolf is called a she-wolf. A baby wolf is called a whelp.

When her whelps are very small, other wolves in the pack bring the she-wolf food so she doesn't have to leave her babies.

A mummy hawk is called a hen.
A baby hawk is called an eyas.

A hen sits on her nest every night
for a whole month, keeping her
eggs safe before they hatch.

A **mummy hare** is called a jill.
A **baby hare** is called a **leveret**.

A leveret is born with fur and
its eyes wide open, ready to
hop around straight away.

A **mummy peacock** is called a **peahen**.
A **baby peacock** is called a **peachick**.

A peachick is born with brown feathers like its mum's. A male peachick will grow its fancy blue feathers at around three years old.

A mummy pig is called a sow.
A baby pig is called a piglet.

A sow sings to her piglets
while she feeds them.

A Lothian Children's Book

Published in Australia and New Zealand in 2020
by Hachette Australia
Level 17, 207 Kent Street, Sydney NSW 2000
www.hachettechildrens.com.au

10 8 6 4 2 3 5 7 9

A catalogue record for this
book is available from the
National Library of Australia

ISBN 978 0 7344 1989 7 (hardback)

Designed by Kinart
Colour reproduction by Splitting Image
Printed in China by Toppan Leefung Printing Limited